Learn My Language! Spanish

Spanish Words at the Zoo

By Nora Dee

Gareth Stevens Publishing

Please visit our website, www.garethstevens.com. For a free color catalog of all our high-quality books, call toll free 1-800-542-2595 or fax 1-877-542-2596.

Library of Congress Cataloging-in-Publication Data

Dee, Nora.
Spanish words at the zoo / by Nora Dee.
 p. cm. — (Learn my language! Spanish)
Includes index.
ISBN 978-1-4824-0358-9 (pbk.)
ISBN 978-1-4824-0359-6 (6-pack)
ISBN 978-1-4824-0355-8 (library binding)
1. Zoo animals — Juvenile literature. 2. Zoos — Juvenile literature. 3. Spanish language — Vocabulary — Juvenile literature. I. Title.
PC4129.E5 D44 2014
468—dc23

First Edition

Published in 2014 by
Gareth Stevens Publishing
111 East 14th Street, Suite 349
New York, NY 10003

Copyright © 2014 Gareth Stevens Publishing

Designer: Sarah Liddell
Editor: Therese Shea

Photo credits: Cover, p. 1 © iStockphoto.com/tiburonstudios; p. 5 Patti McConville/Photographer's Choice/Getty Images; p. 7 Cynthia Kidwell/Shutterstock.com; p. 9 Sally Wallis/Shutterstock.com; p. 11 PeterVrabel/Shutterstock.com; p. 13 Pu Su Lan/Shutterstock.com; p. 15 Tungphoto/Shutterstock.com; p. 17 Four Oaks/Shutterstock.com; p. 19 Vlada Zhykharieva/Shutterstock.com; p. 21 © iStockphoto.com/kali9.

All rights reserved. No part of this book may be reproduced in any form without permission in writing from the publisher, except by a reviewer.

Printed in the United States of America

CPSIA compliance information: Batch #CW14GS: For further information contact Gareth Stevens, New York, New York at 1-800-542-2595.

Contents

Class Trip 4

The Tigers 6

The Lion 8

The Bear 10

Penguins! 12

The Giraffe 14

The Elephant 16

The Alligator 18

Hasta Luego 20

Glossary 22

For More Information 23

Index 24

Boldface words appear in the glossary.

Class Trip

My class is going to the zoo! My teacher will teach us the animals' names in Spanish, or *español*. The Spanish word for zoo is *zoológico*. Look in the box on each page to learn how to say the Spanish words.

Spanish = español (ehs-pah-NYOHL)

zoo = zoológico (soh-oh-LOH-hee-koh)

The Tigers

We go to see the tigers first. The Spanish word for tiger is *tigre*. That's not too hard! There's a cub, too! The Spanish word for cub is *cachorro*.

---

tiger = tigre (TEE-greh)

cub = cachorro (kah-CHOH-rroh)

The Lion

Next, my friend and I go to see the *león*. That's Spanish for lion. The lion has long claws, or *garras*! The *garras* look very sharp!

lion = león (leh-OHN)

claws = garras (GAH-rrahs)

The Bear

It's time to see the *oso*. That's Spanish for bear. Look! The *oso* is swimming in the water, or *agua*. It looks like it's having fun!

bear = oso (OH-soh)

water = agua (AH-gwah)

Penguins!

Penguins are birds, or *pájaros*, that can't fly. The Spanish word for penguin is *pingüino*. The penguins are my favorite animals! What's your favorite animal?

birds = pájaros (PAH-ha-rohs)

penguin = pingüino (peen-GWEE-noh)

The Giraffe

There's the giraffe! The Spanish word for giraffe is *jirafa*. Its neck, or *cuello*, is very, very long. I have to look up to see the *jirafa*'s head! Hello up there!

giraffe = jirafa (hee-RAH-fah)

neck = cuello (KWEH-yoh)

The Elephant

The elephant, or *elefante,* is huge. It has a long *trompa*. That's Spanish for **trunk**. The *elefante* **squirts** water from its *trompa*!

elephant = elefante (eh-leh-FAHN-teh)

trunk = trompa (TROHM-pah)

The Alligator

The alligator, or *caimán*, is the last animal we see. A *caimán* is a **reptile**. All reptiles like to lie in the sun. Look at all those sharp *dientes*! That's Spanish for teeth.

alligator = caimán (Ky-MAHN)

teeth = dientes (DYEN-tehs)

Hasta Luego

We'll come back to the zoo another day to see more animals, or *animales*. We say "*hasta luego*" to all the *animales*. That means "see you later."

animals = animales (ah-nee-MAH-lehs)

see you later = hasta luego (AHS-tah LWEH-goh)

Glossary

reptile: an animal covered with scales or plates that breathes air, has a backbone, and lays eggs, such as a turtle, snake, crocodile, or alligator

squirt: to force something out of a little opening in a quick stream

trunk: the long, bendable nose of an elephant, used for grabbing, feeding, and drinking

For More Information

Books

Berendes, Mary. *Animals = Los Animales.* Mankato, MN: Child's World, 2008.

Clark, Willow. *Lions: Life in the Pride = Leones: Vida en la Manada.* New York, NY: PowerKids Press, 2011.

Mora, Pat. *Marimba! Animales from A to Z.* New York, NY: Clarion Books, 2006.

Websites

Animals You Find at the Zoo
www.spanish-vocabulary.net/zoo-animals.html
Find out how to say more animal names in Spanish.

Zoo Animals Multiple Choice Quiz
www.spanishspanish.com/animals/zoo_multi.html
Take this online Spanish quiz.

Publisher's note to educators and parents: Our editors have carefully reviewed these websites to ensure that they are suitable for students. Many websites change frequently, however, and we cannot guarantee that a site's future contents will continue to meet our high standards of quality and educational value. Be advised that students should be closely supervised whenever they access the Internet.

Index

alligator/caimán 18, 19
animals/animales 20
bear/oso 10, 11
birds/pájaros 12
claws/garras 8, 9
cub/cachorro 6, 7
elephant/elefante 16, 17
giraffe/jirafa 14, 15
lion/león 8, 9
neck/cuello 14, 15
penguin/pingüino 12, 13
see you later/hasta luego 20
Spanish/español 4
teeth/dientes 18, 19
tiger/tigre 6, 7
trunk/trompa 16, 17
water/agua 10, 11
zoo/zoológico 4, 5